TRAINING EXPLAINED

To Mum
with love
from
Mandy.

Training Explained

CAROL GREEN

Ward Lock Limited · London

© Carol Green 1976

First published in Great Britain in 1976
by Ward Lock Limited, 82 Gower Street, London WC1E 6EQ,
a Pentos Company

Reprinted 1979, 1981, 1985

Printed in Great Britain by Hollen Street Press Ltd, Slough.

British Library Cataloguing in Publication Data

Green, Carol
    Training Explained. – (*Horseman's Handbook Series*)
    1. Horses – Training
    I. Title   II. Series
    636.1'083   SF287

    ISBN 0-7063-1971-0 pbk

Contents

Acknowledgments

We are particularly indebted to Brian Young, FBHS, DBHS, Managing Director of Crabbet Park Equitation Centre, Worth, Sussex, (formerly National Instructor at The British Horse Society) and Miss Valerie Lee, BHSI, for help and advice in the preparation of this book; to Miss Marie Stokes, FBHS, Proprietress and Director of Equitation, Walton Heath Livery Stables, Tadworth, Surrey, for her great assistance and technical advice, also for allowing her horses and facilities at Walton Heath to be used for the photographs. To Bob Targett whose photographs have so enriched this publication and to the riders who made this book possible.

Conversion Tables

WEIGHT kilogrammes	kg or pounds	pounds	VOLUME litres	litres or gallons	gallons
0·45	1	2·21	4·55	1	0·22
0·91	2	4·41	9·09	2	0·44
1·36	3	6·61	13·64	3	0·66
1·81	4	8·82	18·18	4	0·88
2·27	5	11·02	22·73	5	1·10
2·72	6	13·23	27·28	6	1·32
3·18	7	15·43	31·82	7	1·54
3·63	8	17·64	36·37	8	1·76
4·08	9	19·84	40·91	9	1·98
4·54	10	22·05	45·46	10	2·20
9·07	20	44·09	90·92	20	4·40
13·61	30	66·14	136·4	30	6·60
18·14	40	88·19	181·8	40	8·80
22·68	50	110·2	227·3	50	11·00
27·22	60	132·3	272·8	60	13·20
31·75	70	154·3	318·2	70	15·40
36·29	80	176·4	363·7	80	17·60
40·82	90	198·4	409·1	90	19·80
45·36	100	220·5	454·6	100	22·00

Temperature Conversion

Celsius -18° -10 0 10 20 30 40°

Fahrenheit 0° 10 20 32 40 50 60 70 80 90 100 110°

$$C = \frac{5}{9}(F - 32) \qquad F = \frac{9}{5}C + 32$$

LIST OF ILLUSTRATIONS   Page

1. Introduction—handling the foal

The term 'breaking' sounds severe and indeed years ago the process of introducing a horse to work was a severe one, with the trainer breaking the horse in too quickly and mainly by sheer physical means. Perhaps a better choice of terms is schooling, or training, which today is achieved by regular handling and patience with progressive training which educates the young horse gradually.

If a trainer is to achieve good results when schooling a horse he should possess certain qualities, the most important ones being:

  patience
  understanding
  sympathy, coupled with firmness
  good temper
  thoughtfulness
  ability resulting from study, observation and practice

Our training system must be governed by certain principles, the horse learning by the association of ideas—habit; the most important principle is that of reward and correction. When the horse does well he is rewarded immediately with a pat on the neck or a few softly spoken words, whereas when he needs correcting, either the lesson is repeated or he is spoken to firmly. The horse must be given favourable opportunities to learn with the time, place and location right for the task. All training must be carried out on progressive lines in a systematic way with each new lesson introduced towards the end of the training session but while the horse is still mentally and physically capable. All lessons should end on a good note. Throughout his training the horse must have sufficient food for his physical development and to enable him to do what we ask but not so much that he becomes over-excited or too fat.

Training should begin from the earliest possible age—ideally with the foal—almost from birth, so that the very young horse develops confidence, a feeling of security, and learns obedience from the start. A foal that is handled sympathetically from birth makes life easier for himself and his trainer. He should be haltered at a very early age, within a week of birth if possible, as the longer he is left without handling the more difficult it is to fit the halter when you wish to begin training. It is natural for the youngster to become a little excited when first handled, so to avoid possible accident I suggest that you adopt the following procedure.

The foal and his dam should be in a loose box with a deep bed of clean straw with well-banked sides in order to avoid the risk of injury. The foal should be patted gently all over and have his feet picked up and held as a rehearsal for the time when a farrier will do this. A leather foal slip (small headcollar) which has a cross-strap adjustment at the back, fits snugly and does not slide, should be put on very gently in the stable. When he is accustomed to the foal slip he should be ready to lead in hand. These preparations may take several days but do not be in a hurry and try to rush them.

To lead the foal with his mother, two people, the trainer and an assistant, will be needed. The assistant should lead the mare while the trainer leads the foal. The trainer should be at the foal's shoulder leading him by a long, light lead rein close to the mare. If he should prove difficult to lead place a hand round his hindquarters and say 'walk on'—always repeating the same words, so that he will learn to understand what this means—as an order. Initially he should be led with his mother but gradually he should be coaxed away from her to be led on his own. It is important to handle the foal on both sides from the start, so that he learns to be led from both sides by the trainer, with the latter making large circles (of about sixty feet in diameter) to left and right, otherwise the foal may develop what is known as a 'stiff side'—that is, a dislike for turning either to the left or to the right. It is to be hoped that the mother is easy to catch and handle because the foal will learn more easily by imitating her, the foal feeling more secure in his dam's presence.

It may be necessary for the foal to travel when accompanying the mare, either to a horse show or to stud. Normallly the mare will revisit the stallion seven to ten days after foaling, unless there have been foaling complications, and her foal will travel with his dam, not being left at home. This is good training for the future, accustoming the foal to the actual travelling, to unfamiliar sights and sounds and to being led in hand. It is, of

10

course, preferable to have your own transport so that he can be trained at home by being encouraged into box or trailer daily. Assuming you have your own trailer, remove the partition so that the mare and her foal can travel in the whole box. Training in loading and travelling can then be carried out at home so long as you have an experienced person to help you. Never try to do anything for the first time with a young horse without someone experienced to advise you. For this familiarising process of loading it is important to ensure that the box stands firmly on level ground with the end, at which you load him, placed in such a way to get as much light into the box as possible.

Make the whole experience of loading as pleasant as possible for the young horse by giving him a reward in the shape of a small feed when he is in the trailer. Then he can be led out when your assistant has lowered the front ramp.

When the foal is walking confidently into the trailer or box, and appears unfussed, it is time to take him on a short journey. He will travel loose in the box with his mother. Drive with extreme caution and do watch out for overhanging tree

A pony dressed in a woollen rug for travelling in winter

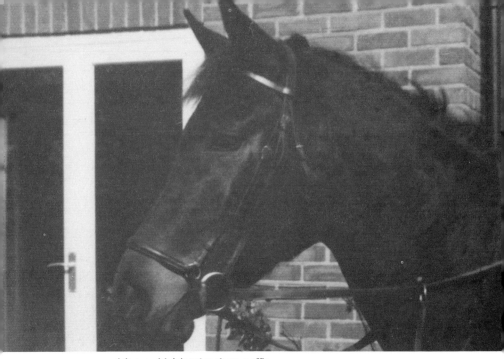

A horse with jointed eggbutt snaffle

branches which may make an unpleasant rattling on the roof of the box. It goes without saying that you should try to avoid the possibility of getting into noisy traffic at this stage—your foal has to become accustomed to strange and disturbing sounds but the process should be made as gradual as possible on these early 'dummy runs'.

In the young horse's first year little formal training will be given. The year should be used to develop confidence in his trainer when being caught in the field, led into his stable and tied up, when having his feet picked up, lightly groomed all over and moving over in the stable when he is told. Monthly visits from the blacksmith are a good preparation—he will get used to having his feet trimmed and will not be so nervous about shoes being fitted when the time comes.

The yearling and the two-year-old should learn to obey the trainer's spoken orders both in and out of the stable. He should walk in hand to the command 'walk on' and to trot—to 'trot on' equally well from both sides. For this last he may wear a small snaffle bit. When you fit a bit for the first time warm it so that the metal is not cold on the horse's mouth and smear the mouthpiece with a little honey or treacle to divert his attention from the metal you have put into his mouth. Leave him standing for a few minutes with the bridle on while he is in the stable but stay with him yourself in case he gets upset.

A useful method of introducing the youngster to traffic on his home ground is to take him near stationary vehicles which have their engines running. When he is quite used to them, he can be taken on lanes around his home where he will encounter light traffic. He should, at this stage, be introduced to as many different sights and sounds as possible in such a way that he is not startled—always having the presence of his trainer with comforting voice and hand to reassure him.

If your yearling or two-year-old is considered suitable for showing this would prove useful experience for him. Before he is shown, however, he must wear a snaffle bridle, be confident in loading and travelling, lead well in hand—and of course stand well. Such basic ring experience will give your horse the opportunity to see and hear those sights and sounds which he may expect as a show horse in later times and to work in the company of other horses and people.

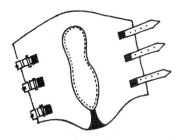

Brushing boot

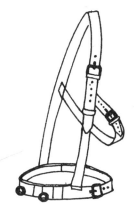

Lungeing cavesson

2. Equipment for the three-year-old

A young horse is still growing and developing muscle and bone until well into his fifth year and so it is not wise to ask too much of him at a very early age. At three he should be introduced to being ridden — 'backed'. Basic familiarisation and training can be accomplished but the intensive training should not begin until he comes from his field—after a rest in the spring when he is four. The essential features of that 'familiarisation' mentioned above are, of course, his equipment.

Brushing boots—four

These are a protective covering of felt, leather or rubber wrapped around the lower legs, held on by leather or velcro straps which, when fitted, protect the youngster's legs should he knock them by brushing one against the other, when he could be injured or suffer permanent blemish.

Lungeing cavesson

It should be of strong leather and fit snugly and, for the purpose to be described, should have a centre ring which swivels.

Lungeing rein

The webbing lungeing rein should be at least thirty feet long. This allows you to work the horse on a large circle. The line

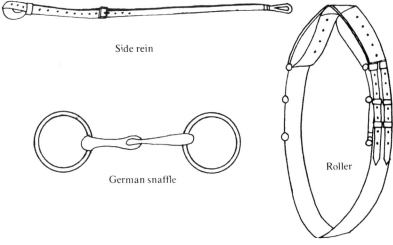

Side rein

German snaffle

Roller

Training should begin from the earliest possible age —▶
ideally from the foal

should also have a swivel fitted so that there is less risk of it becoming twisted as you work.

Long driving reins
These should be twenty-five feet in length and made of lightweight webbing. The first eight feet from the bit should be of rolled leather or half-inch rope which allows the rein to slip easily through the D's, rings, or terrets of the lungeing roller.

Side reins
One pair of adjustable leather side reins with spring clips to attach them to the cavesson and, later, to the bit rings.

Gloves
Always wear gloves for training as well as for riding. In training, a horse can pull hard at you and badly burn your hands through the friction of webbing, rope or leather. Lightweight leather gloves are the most suitable.

Lunge whip
These vary in length but choose one that is well balanced and not too heavy.

Lungeing roller
A well-padded leather roller is best for your purpose and, of course, it should be kept oiled and supple. It should have three rings on each side to enable you to vary the height of the long reins and side reins.

Bit
As all but the rawest novices know, the bit is that piece of the horse's equipment which goes into his mouth; the best suited to this stage of the horse's training is a German snaffle, which has a thick but light mouthpiece or, as an alternative, you can use a rubber snaffle. The only disadvantage of the latter, however, is that since it is straight barred, a young horse may curl his tongue back over the top of the bit. I consider bits with mouthing keys, that is bits with key-shaped pieces of metal attached for the young horse to play with, unnecessary, tending to make the horse fussy and unsettled in his mouth.

Handling and leading the foal (next to the mother)

Leading the foal with hand behind the quarters

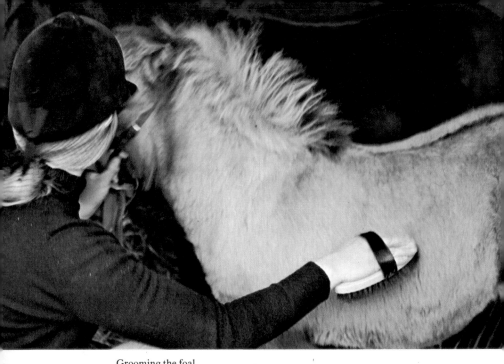

Grooming the foal

Leading the three-year-old in hand in a snaffle and bridle with schooling whip

First lunge lesson wearing bridle, brushing boots and cavesson

Wearing a roller (notice the piece of foam underneath the roller to ensure maximum comfort)

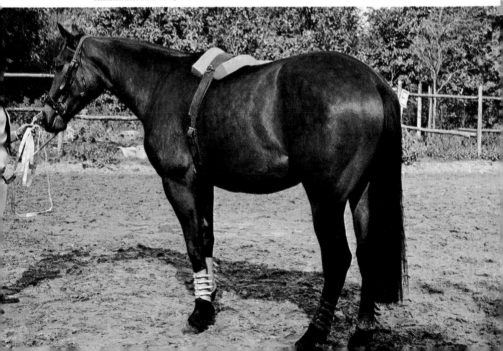

Lungeing the horse with saddle and surcingle fitted; the stirrups are hanging loose so that the horse becomes used to the irons dangling before mounting

Leaning across the horse in the stable

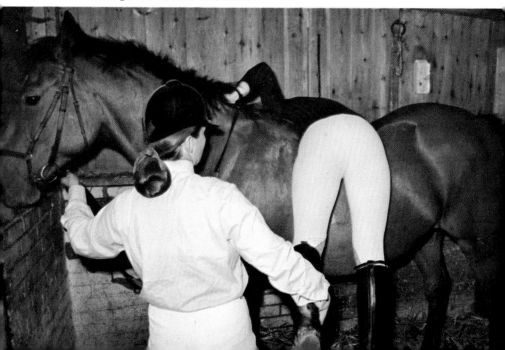

Dressage or schooling whip

This item of your equipment will be valuable throughout the training of the young horse—in fact it is essential to trainer and horse and is used even when the trainee is walked in hand so that he learns to work from whip and voice. Proper use of the whip will result in the horse answering to the trainer as well without a rider as when he is working with a rider. The correct use of a dressage whip is to touch the horse very lightly with the end two inches of the whip only by a slight flick of the trainer's wrist.

Each item of equipment should be fitted by an experienced person to ensure maximum comfort for the horse.

With regard to training-space facilities, a well-kept indoor school is to be preferred but is not absolutely essential. However, an enclosure with a level surface—a *manège*—is essential. Good hacking country and some simple jumping equipment, which I will describe later, should also be available.

A well-equipped tack room

3. Training the three-year-old

The horse should, by now, be well-mannered and easy to handle in the stable. Keep his brushing boots on for an hour each day so that he gets used to wearing them but let him move around in the stable while they are on before leaving him alone, because if he is not thoroughly accustomed to the boots he may kick at his box and perhaps injure himself.

Leading in hand

If you have had your horse since a foal you will have taught him to lead in hand, but if he is a new purchase I suggest that he is also taught to be led in hand on both reins to become familiar with his surroundings.

He is taught in a similar manner to that adopted when teaching the foal, but he will be alone. He must learn to lead well from both sides, stand still, trot while being led and turn round, be familiar with light traffic, stand quietly tied up in the stable, become accustomed to wearing brushing boots, a rug and roller whilst in the stable.

Lungeing

After a week, lungeing may begin, the horse wearing brushing boots on all four legs, a lungeing cavesson, a bridle and lungeing rein, with the trainer wearing gloves, as already advised.

Lungeing is beneficial to the horse in that it helps to develop suppleness, balance, muscles, co-ordination and obedience. As horses learn by habit all training must be systematic. To start lungeing your young horse you should have an assistant to lead the horse round while you stand at the centre of the circle holding the lunge rein and giving your words of command. As the horse responds to the trainer's command to walk on, he should walk a circle with the trainer encouraging him forwards. Continue on a circle, taking care not to get in front of the horse. The prime factor here is that the trainee is learning to respond to the trainer's voice, the whip and lungeing rein aids coming from the trainer's hand, so that he learns to travel on a circle with a light contact with the lungeing rein. All work must be done by the trainer equally on both reins and for this first lungeing lesson five minutes is ample for the novice horse.

During this exercise, as in all others, it goes without saying that a calm voice, backed by firm actions, will give the horse confidence.If, while lungeing, you wish to slow the horse down, use the time-honoured 'whoa, whoa', quietly and gently, and when progressing from a walk to a trot, speak only a little sharper with 'trot, trot', then slow him down as before when a walk is required.

As in the case of most domestic animals, it is not *what* you say but the way in which you say it—tone is more important than the actual word used. The faster the pace required, the more positive and higher the voice; the slower the pace, the softer and lower the tone.

Lungeing correctly is difficult, so before trying to educate a young horse on the lunge, gain experience by practising with an experienced horse which lunges well. Always have a knowledgeable person standing by to give you advice.

Points to remember when lungeing a young horse:

1 Always work on as large a circle as possible, approximately sixty feet in diameter, so that you put the minimum strain on

A horse with a rubber snaffle

the horse's hind legs. Small circles will adversely affect them—particularly the hocks.

2 Two or three minutes' lungeing on each rein is sufficient at first, gradually increasing to about five minutes on each rein twice at the end of about two weeks. Many horses' natural paces are shortened and impaired through lungeing for too long and on too small a circle.

3 To cultivate a pleasant working association between trainer and horse, the trainer should reward the 'pupil' at the end of each lesson by halting the horse, going out to him on the circle and giving him a pat on the neck while telling him that he has done well. Never allow the horse to come in to you as he may do it when you do not want him to.

4 At this stage respect for the lunge whip must be established as the horse must never be frightened of the whip. It is used behind the horse in the direction of his hocks to drive him forwards, with an upwards flick towards the girth to encourage him to move more energetically and towards the shoulder to indicate to him to keep out on the circle.

An important rule to observe through each phase of schooling the very young horse is never to pass from one step to another until you are sure that each lesson has been absorbed. If you adhere to this ruling you will find that your trainee will be schooled calmly and without fuss. The fuss will come at some later stage if indeed the horse has not been thoroughly schooled at each successive step.

If the young horse has now come to understand the work on the lunge and is accustomed to wearing boots, bridle and cavesson, then he can be fitted with a roller. This piece of equipment has already been briefly explained. Its fitting can be disturbing for the young horse, so I suggest that after working him with the lunge rein as usual, you take him to the stable where a deep bed has been laid. As before, have an experienced person to help you. Your assistant should hold the horse, talking soothingly to him so that he stays confident and comforted. You, as the trainer, should also talk to him in a soothing way while gently fitting the roller, being careful not to do it up too tightly. Once it is on, the horse should be allowed to move around in the stable—being able to breathe out while feeling this new equipment around his middle. This is an important part of the horse's schooling because many youngsters who have been carelessly and roughly treated beforehand prove difficult to girth up or fit with the roller. The youngster should not be left unattended after this fitting because should he take fright while wearing the roller for the first time, he could injure himself by dashing around the stable and knocking himself. When the horse has grown accustomed to the roller in his stable he can be lunged in the *manège* with it on. As he works in the trot, the roller will become tighter and so be prepared for him to buck or become excited. Calm him all the time by talking to him gently as he works through any upset. When he has learnt to lunge well on both reins while wearing the roller, the time has come to teach him to 'long rein'.

Long-reining

The tack to fit now is bridle, cavesson, roller and long reins. One rein is fitted to the ring on the near side of the cavesson, the other to the offside ring and then passed through the centre ring, or terret, of the roller. Work the horse on the left rein to begin with, lungeing him in the usual way and allowing him to get used to the right rein, just keeping it loose and lying across his back. The horse should be worked at the walk. If he accepts and understands this lesson on the left rein, then reverse the procedure and work on the right rein. Simply reverse the reins so the right is the lunge rein and the left the support rein, just passing through the terrets, until you find that the horse is going well on the lunge circle, accepting the second rein.

As with all new experiences, this may take several days for the young horse to accept. Throughout this period you should have a knowledgeable person with you to give help and advice, if needed. Remember that this, like every lesson, must have been absorbed by the horse to the trainer's complete satisfaction before passing to the next stage.

The horse should feel relaxed on long reins—he should be at ease while the reins lie on his back or touch his quarters. If the horse is at all apprehensive he should be handled all over with the reins in a soothing manner while at halt.

In these early lessons on long reins it is preferable to use an enclosed space such as an indoor school or *manège*, so that it the horse should pull away from the trainer it is possible to regain control promptly. Sometimes a young horse will panic if he finds himself loose, with reins trailing. For this reason, with a horse of nervous temperament, do not pass the inside rein through the 'D' or terret but have it direct to the cavesson, so that should anything go wrong, it will be a simple matter to drop the outside rein and lunge the horse on a circle to regain control.

The closer the trainer is to the horse, the better the control. The aim is to have the lightest possible contact on the reins, working for a regular rhythm at all paces. The hand must maintain a contact on the rein all the time without any backward tension, the same principle being applied in all correct equitation. The horse must be made to go forwards, 'taking', or accepting, the rein, not forced by a hand pulling back.

As soon as the horse is able to walk and trot on the long reins calmly and confidently, he will be ready to begin work with both reins correctly fitted through their appropriate terrets. The advantages of long-reining are that the horse is able to work on straight lines and circles from an early stage in training, make transitions and changes of direction. This will render him more supple and athletic.

If by now the young horse has been well-handled and exercised, and feels confident with his trainer, it is time to introduce him to the saddle. A linen-lined saddle, provided the lining is clean and not lumpy, is best for our purpose since it will be less cold to the young horse's back than one which is leather-lined. The saddle, without stirrup irons and leathers, should first be put on in the stable, making sure that it is well forward, with the youngster's hair lying flat, and that there is no risk of pinching or discomfort. The girth should be fastened loosely for the first two or three fittings, gradually drawing it a little more firmly on each successive saddling-up. Since the horse has been working with a roller fitted, this fastening of the girth should cause no problems.

When the young horse appears to have accepted the saddle and seems accustomed to the feel of it, he should be walked around the stable with it on so that he will also become used to its firmness when he is moving.

Never leave a young horse alone in the stable with his new saddle on in case something should frighten him and, in panic, he should buck and injure himself in the box.

The next stage in training will be the working of the horse on the lunge line while he is wearing his saddle. For this I would fit a surcingle over the top of the saddle to prevent it from slipping and worrying the horse. The saddled horse is now worked on the lunge as before—at 'walk' and 'trot'—and when all has gone well and the trainer is quite satisfied that the saddle is in no way affecting his performance, the next stage is to fit stirrup irons and leathers to the saddle but to secure the stirrups to the girth so that he will not be frightened by their dangling loosely and hitting his sides. Lead the horse about and move the irons and leathers while handling him before lungeing with the irons and leathers dangling. When the horse has worked thus, obediently and calmly, the stirrups can be released and allowed to touch his sides during his lessons so that he becomes used to them. This is a valuable part of his 'backing' training because should he and any future rider he may have part company, he will not be startled by the touch of loose irons and the flapping of leathers.

'Backing' the horse

Backing is the colloquial term for a horse being mounted by a rider, and carrying a rider for the first time. The preparations for this very important part of the young horse's training should be made in the stable after exercise on the lunge. Here the youngster feels secure and the trainer has more control in the enclosed area. A deep straw bed should be provided, lessening the risk of any injury to the horse or rider. Remove water bucket, haynet and manger—if portable—before proceeding. Normal routine should have been established during grooming and leading up to this backing. The trainer's assistant should work with firmness, gradually putting more and more pressure on the horse's back while the trainer holds the horse and, with one hand, lifts the assistant to a progressively higher and higher position until he leans across the horse. When the horse has accepted this arrangement calmly your assistant allows his or her weight to bear down slightly on the horse's saddle area while the trainer is holding the head and comforting the horse. This pressure is increased until gradually the horse is taking the assistant's full weight. Finally the latter, a lightweight of course, should be able to

28

slip a leg over and actually sit on the horse. This should be carried out gradually and on both sides of the horse, the trainer at all times keeping control from the head.

When the trainer is confident that the horse has accepted this preliminary carrying of weight and actual mounting in the stable, the horse should be mounted in the *manège*.

Lungeing in this way will enable the rider to obtain a deeper seat

4. Riding the horse in the manège

This should be done after the horse has been worked. As before, your assistant should be a lightweight, be known to the horse through grooming it and be a reasonably proficient rider. This is important because any nervous tension on the part of the person mounting the horse will be instantly conveyed to the young horse. The trainer, in whom the horse should have complete confidence by now, stays at the horse's shoulder. The assistant should first lie across the saddle, as before in the stable, and do so from both sides, and the horse should then be walked a few yards with the assistant in this position, accustoming the horse to this unusual weight and enabling him to adjust his balance to carry it. Reward the horse at every stage by giving him a gentle pat on the neck.

The next step can be taken when the horse is seen to be accepting this in a calm and relaxed manner. He should, of course, be brought to a halt, after walking a few steps, for the 'rider' to get off. Pat the horse at every stage. Your assistant

Taking a 'leg up' in the *manège*

should next mount by means of a 'leg up' — first lying across the saddle — high, towards the neck; then, keeping low on the horse, gently bringing over the right leg to sit astride. The rider should sit quite still, pat the horse, talking quietly and comfortingly all the time. The horse should be wearing a neck strap for this mounting so that there is no risk of the rider instinctively drawing on the reins to maintain his balance should the horse become startled.

The trainer should lunge the horse at the outset of this introduction to a rider while the rider uses his voice to encourage the horse to go forwards. The horse must learn to stand still when mounted, to go from walk to trot and then back to walk quietly and calmly. These transitions of pace will be carried out to begin with by the horse responding to the trainer's voice, but from these very early mounted lessons the youngster is taught gradually to respond to the rider's leg, as the basis of all equitation is free forward movement. The horse must be given a definite aid, the rider gently but firmly using his legs in the girth area at the horse's sides. The voice should be used to reassure the horse, encouraging him to go forwards.

Lying across the horse in the *manège*

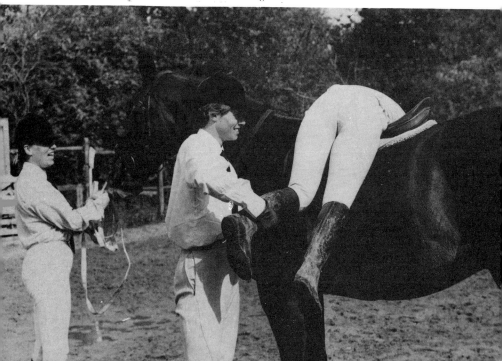

These early lessons, in an enclosed space, should be for short periods only. The young horse will tire quickly and the trainer must be careful not to overtax him. Five minutes a day for two or three days is sufficient, gradually increasing to twenty minutes twice a day by the end of four weeks.

It is beneficial for the young horse to be lunged daily for a few minutes without a rider, as young horses tend to be high-spirited and also cannot carry the rider's weight for long periods. Gradually, as the horse becomes more accustomed to carrying the rider, the lungeing can be dispensed with. The horse will benefit from working on straight lines, being ridden energetically forwards at the walk and trot and then into halt. A few turns and large circles of about sixty feet in diameter may be commenced, with the rider maintaining a light contact on the reins.

Teaching the horse to respond to aids, or signals
Communication between horse and rider is achieved with aids. These aids are, briefly, the use of the rider's seat, legs, hands, voice and body weight. These are called natural aids while

Sitting on. (Notice that the rider holds the neck strap and is without stirrups)

artificial aids include whips, spurs and martingales; with the young horse the only artificial aid needed is the whip.

With these aids the trainer can indicate to the horse what is required of him. In his stable the horse learns to move over during grooming by the trainer pressing his hand to the horse's side at the same time saying 'over'—soon the horse responds to the pressure of the trainer's hand and moves over; when the horse shows that he understands, by obeying this hand and voice command, he should be rewarded with a pat.

In teaching the horse such aids the trainer is all the time developing the horse's response to touch and voice and later the advanced horse will react to the chief means of communication from the rider — that of touch — with or without voice. The reactions of the trained horse will be to the rider's seat, legs and hands.

The aids for slowing down or stopping are the rider's legs and hands, and the weight of his or her body. The good rider will have developed a natural instinctive feel for the horse's movements and thus will anticipate and prevent any evasions by the use of his legs in conjunction with 'giving and taking' on the reins.

I have found that in the early stages of teaching the horse to respond to my leg, one of the best ways is by using a schooling whip and the voice, so that with 'walk on' the whip should be lightly flicked in the area of the horse's girth and at the same time the calves vibrated in the girth area — thus using three aids. Gradually, as the horse begins to understand these signals I dispense with the voice — then later with the whip — until the horse responds just to that vibration of my calves. In this way it is possible to train the novice horse to be responsive to leg aids without fuss or resistance.

When the horse is responding well to simple aids it is a good idea to commence hacking through the lanes with an older and more experienced horse. This stage of his training should be taken over a period of six months during the first year after the horse has been backed.

It is unwise to lunge the young horse or work him on small circles—that is to say circles which are less than forty feet in diameter—for any length of time because muscle and bone for such exercises are not yet developed. The result will be too much strain on the hocks and forelegs. The young horse must be encouraged to go forward calmly, adjusting his balance without being 'held up' by the trainer's hand, thus avoiding strain to his limbs. During this work the trainer must also see that the horse's energy comes from his hindquarters, this being the essence of good training and free forward movement. Much knowledge of the individual horse can be gained by riding across country at all paces, both in company and alone. The trainer teaches the horse to adjust to his balance and renders him a safe performer over all kinds of ground.

In the horse's fourth year he is ready to begin working on turns, circles and transitions, all of which add to his suppleness, athletic ability and balance. The latter is most important. Before a horse begins training he has, of course, natural balance but once he is mounted he has to adjust his balance to include the weight and movements of a rider. In his natural state a young horse puts two-thirds of his weight on his front legs while grazing. The trainer has to encourage the horse to bring his point of balance back so that each hind leg takes its share of the weight which should be distributed in such a way that complete balance with the rider is achieved. When a youngster becomes apprehensive and is preparing to move away at speed, he first raises his head. His weight is then moved back and his hind legs come under him in a collected position. When he extends, his head is well out and forward. The trainer must strive to improve the horse's fluid balance which is accomplished by the moving of the horse's centre of gravity forward and back without jolting rider or horse. The horse should thus become more comfortable in his movement, not overtaxing any one leg or part of his body. This fluid balance is the means by which the trainer achieves rhythm in movement.

So far as equitation is concerned, good rhythm is the regular step of a horse at all paces — uniformity of a good stride.

Do not try schooling intensively until the horse reaches four years old—this is quite young enough. It is sufficient to have hacked him for gentle riding along the lanes with an older horse, and have both horse and trainer enjoying such outings, when he is three years old, then turn him out to grow and develop for the formal training of the next year.

5. Turning out the three-year-old

Fencing or hedges must be sound and adequate for the size of the horse, for while a pony will push at an unsound section of hedging and get through, a horse will jump a fence which is inadequate in height. A post and rail fence is the most suitable but is also the most expensive. A thick hedge, well-maintained, perhaps with a clean ditch, is also quite adequate. Any kind of fencing constructed mainly of wire should be avoided. Both horses and ponies tend to get themselves caught up in the wire and can injure themselves.

A good supply of fresh water is essential — a running stream or properly tended water trough. In winter it is important to check that the water is not too iced up for the horse to drink. The field should also be tidy, with no broken glass, bottles or cans, or any kind of rubbish on which the horse or pony can injure himself. Young horses are naturally inquisitive about strange objects so be careful to check the field daily and clear away anything which may prove dangerous.

Poisonous plants, such as deadly nightshade — or belladonna, ragwort, ivy or yew — must not be present in your horse's field. It may be wise to obtain a handbook to help identify these if there is any doubt because they can have fatal results. When you are sure that you can identify such plants, carefully inspect the field and hedges to make certain there are none there.

Wind-breaks, provided by high hedges, trees or a wooden shelter — field shelter — are welcome, even in summer when it provides the horse with protection from flies. In winter the advantages are obvious.

Make sure that there is no mud around the gateway, water trough or at that spot where a horse may drink from running water because when such mud freezes into hard and uneven shapes it will prove a discomfort, if not actually a hazard, to both the horse and yourself. Thus gates should be sited on the highest part of the grazing land, where they will be drained naturally. Try not to have a water trough situated too near a gate because with several horses accommodated in the same field the area will become worn and muddy, with horses going to the trough or being taken out for shoeing, grooming or exercise.

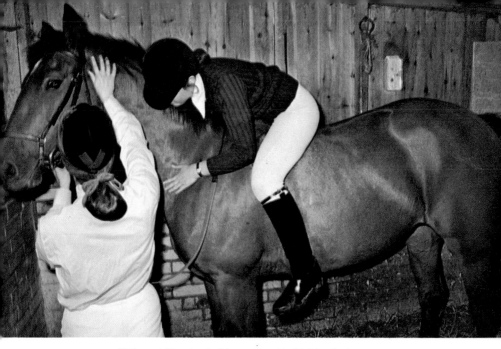

Sitting astride, crouched low so as not to frighten the horse

Walking the horse with rider lying across the saddle

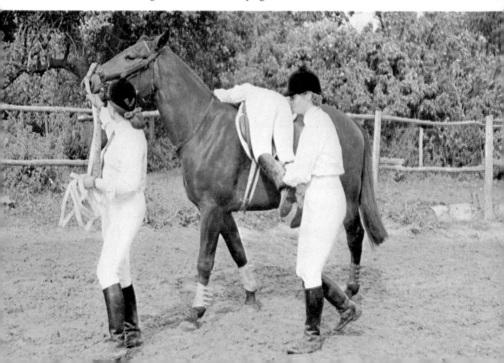

Lungeing the rider with stirrups

Teaching the horse to respond to the aids by use of schooling whip

Walking over ground rails

Trotting over ground rails

A horse at grass should be inspected daily for any cuts or other injuries which may need attention. Such a daily check should ideally include inspection of hedge or fencing for any breaks or dangerous protrusions.

If the three-year-old has been backed and initially schooled in the summer, then his rest time under the above circumstances will probably be from September to the following April. Grass alone does not contain sufficient nutriment for a youngster in training, and although he may not be doing any work, he must be fed hay and corn.

If the horse is a finely-bred specimen—such as a Thorough-bred—he may lose condition by being out constantly during the winter and so should be comfortably stabled each night and only turned out during the day for exercise. In this way the horse gets the maximum benefit from his freedom at grass and a warm shelter with corn feed.

If a horse is 'turned away' completely in winter he must have two 'hard' feeds daily, plus as much hay as he wants. Remember that a horse's feed requirement varies with the individual, according to his age, size and temperament as well as the amount of work he is expected to do. For a horse of fifteen hands about six pounds of concentrates and twelve pounds of hay will be the average daily requirement.

6. Conditioning the four-year-old

Lessons of the previous year should have been absorbed by the four-year-old and he should now go much better. First, however, the youngster's body must be conditioned for the work we are going to expect him to do. After his long rest from formal training, it will take approximately six weeks to get the horse into sufficiently hard condition.

If you have fed him those 'hard feeds' daily, as described above, a change in diet should not occasion too much adjustment for him. There are, however, problems which may arise if he does not receive close care and attention in his first few days of coming 'off grass'. At this time horses are prone to 'filled legs' (swelling of the lower legs) and 'humour spots' (small lumps under the skin).

To prevent both of these ailments, which are caused by over-feeding, any additional concentrates (hard food) should be introduced and increased gradually according to the amount of work the horse is being given. All feeds should be given slightly dampened with water. Hay should also be fed damp by tipping a little water over it and then leaving for an hour or so to allow the water to drain from it. Dampening the food in this way helps to prevent coughing caused by dust in the food.

In these first days 'off grass' a horse may get coughs, colds or sore throats because of the change of surroundings and diet. To guard against these, ensure that the horse has plenty of fresh air by leaving the top half of the stable door open at all times.

The horse should have only light exercise at first with no risk of sweating with the consequent loss of condition. For the first week lead the horse in hand and begin lungeing for two sessions of about ten minutes each day so that the horse is out of his stable for two periods of work to avoid tiredness and boredom. If possible, throughout his training, turn him out in the field for at least an hour every day.

A horse out of condition can easily get a sore back or a girth gall. These are rubs from the saddle or girth and can be avoided by hardening the skin in these areas. Dress the areas touched by the equipment with a solution of salt and water every day. It is possible that while the horse's saddle fitted him well enough when he was first backed, it may not fit as well now as he comes from grass, so repeat the process of his first backing, making sure that the saddle does not pinch. Ask a knowledgeable person to help you with the fitting of the saddle and bridle. Having led your trainee in hand and, in the first week, lunged him for ten minutes at a time, continue during the second and third weeks, gradually increasing his ridden exercise so that by the end of the third week he can begin roadwork for up to half an hour daily. Steady work on the roads helps to strengthen tendons. Also trotting work can be introduced but it is sufficient to begin with two minutes at a time.

In his ridden roadwork, always with that older, more experienced horse to steady him, the young horse is becoming more and more accustomed to sights and sounds different from those he will have seen and heard out at grass on his home ground. Progress from all this can be made in the fourth and fifth weeks with an introduction to some slight hill work, to improve the trainee's wind and strengthen his back. It also makes him use his shoulders and helps him to adjust his balance with a rider on his back.

If all has gone well during the first five weeks, in the sixth week some cantering can be introduced with walk, trot, canter, for up to one and a half hours a day. Throughout this period I would have been reducing the quantities of bulk foods and increasing the concentrates until the proportions are approximately half bulk and half concentrates, so that by the seventh and eighth weeks the horse should be ready to begin basic work with schooling without taxing his strength or risking strain. The four-year-old should have become quite accustomed to regular grooming and trimming which is described later. The farrier should have paid him several visits, first to trim his feet and then to fit his first shoes. If this, and the putting on of rugs, bandages and boots, has been accomplished with patience and sympathy, the horse should be calm and tractable. An important rule is never to leave your horse wearing something which is unfamiliar to him. See that the wearing of his boots and any flapping of a rug causes him no distress. If all preparatory stages have been made to your

own and your horse's apparent satisfaction before moving on to other stages in his schooling, you will save yourself trouble in the future.

Success in all early lessons depends on the trainer's own 'horse-sense' with sympathetically firm handling. Incorrect handling and impatient treatment will spoil the most promising horse. No matter how good you may think your horse will be ultimately, if you have not developed that 'horse-sense' and a working rapport with your youngster, he will be spoiled; not 'spoiled' in the sense that he is pampered, but spoiled for the kind of formal riding for which you hope to train him. This is why it is so important to have a knowledgeable person present whenever you attempt a new lesson. That working rapport, gained by tact, kindness, patience and firmness, begins as you enter the stable. Speak softly with an encouraging tone; horses are most susceptible to the timbre of a human voice.

Approach from the near side, going towards the horse's shoulder, patting him lightly while talking. Do not rush the approach or bustle about him at any time. All hasty, sudden movements and noise must be avoided in the presence of a youngster as this will confuse and unnerve him. When you are grooming, try standing as close as possible to your horse; this gives him confidence and of course there is less chance of your getting hurt by some sudden move on his part. The end of a kick, or strike, is the most painful point in the delivery of it but if you are close to the horse, with that kick only beginning, it becomes only a push, which will result in no serious hurt.

When you have completed that first approach to the horse's shoulder, put on his halter or headcollar and tie him up. You have approached on the near side, speaking to the horse and lightly patting him, now slip the headcollar rope around his neck and with your left hand you can put on the headcollar, positioning the noseband first, then fastening the buckle between poll and cheekbone, using both hands of course. When tying up use a 'quick release knot'; a knot which comes undone immediately you pull the end of the rope.

If all the foregoing preliminaries have been observed when the youngster comes off grass after his rest, he should now be fit enough to begin a more intensive training programme.

◀ Farrier at work. Frequent checks should be made on shoes which should be renewed every 4-6 weeks on average

7. Basic training for the four-year-old

In order that the horse may improve in suppleness and obedience through these early lessons, it is necessary for the trainer to be conversant with simple schooling movements used in training the young horse on the flat. These movements should render him obedient to the rider's leg aids. This is important in a young horse, whether he is being trained for jumping or for dressage.

The horse must only be made to work on a single track, that is to say when the hindleg movements follow the foreleg movements with the rider changing direction and going the opposite way, riding loops, circles, serpentines and changes of direction within the circle; see examples opposite.

Diagrams of simple movements; there are many more than these:

1 Turn down the centre line to change the rein
2 Turn across the school to change the rein
3 Single shallow loop
4 Inverted loop or changing the rein out of the corner followed by changing the rein into the corner
5 Three loops of the serpentine
6 Incline across the school
7 Large circle
8 Changing the rein out of the circle
9 Changing the rein within the circle
10 Half circle and incline back to the track
11 Turn down the centre line and incline back to the track
12 Half circle across the school

These movements are best practised at a walk because both rider and horse will find them easier to perform at a slow pace. As balance and agility improve then proceed to the trot. The horse should be trained to bend in the direction of the movement to be executed with plenty of changes of direction as in the examples above.

If at the beginning the horse does not appear to answer the leg aids, by all means encourage with the voice in much the same

way as in lungeing. A horse may lose energy or impulsion on the turns or changes of direction and the rider must anticipate this and ride energetically and firmly, maintaining rhythm of stride. This also maintains impulsion, which comes from the rear, and prevents the horse from shortening his stride on the turns.

I have found it helpful to the horse to lunge him two or three times a week before starting on mounted work—lungeing, that is, with the saddle on, making the horse circle and complete wide turns without losing his pace, rhythm and impulsion.

The trainer should now progress from lungeing to working on improving the horse's transitions—increase and decrease of pace—both on a loose rein and with rein contact. It is advisable to work the horse on a loose rein so that he does not always depend on the rider's hand. In this way the young horse develops self-carriage—the ability to carry himself without relying on the rider's hands—while maintaining the same outline of his neck and back, and a regular rhythm in his stride. I would suggest that at this stage the trainer can move on to some initial work with ground rails. These poles should be placed on the ground approximately four feet apart for ponies, four feet six inches apart for horses of fourteen to fifteen hands, up to four feet eight inches for horses over fifteen hands. Ground rails help the horse to look down to the ground whilst maintaining a regular rhythm in his stride and encouraging him to use the muscles in his back correctly. With these exercises, always be aware of the horse's condition and remember that he must be fit to make it possible for his body to harden as muscles are developed.

Ground rail work helps to develop the horse's fitness provided he is getting a proper balance between the right type of food and this exercise.

When working with ground rails it is preferable to begin with one and, when the horse is moving calmly over it, increase to three at a time. Begin work at a regularly paced walk, letting the horse adjust his balance while the rider maintains the lightest rein contact. The horse should not be 'held up' by the rider's hands. When the horse has gained confidence just walking over the rails, he can be made to trot over, still with the lightest rein contact. At this stage the poles must be actually on the ground—raised poles, or cavalletti, can be dangerous. When a young horse is made to trot over even slightly raised poles, his muscles are being put under too much strain. I have seen horses suffer from unnecessary injury through being made to work in this exaggerated style while still too young.

In these initial lessons it is important to keep a definite aim in mind so that at each stage you feel that you have kept the confidence of your trainee—a confidence which has been gained by degrees. It is important for the youngster to enjoy all his work. Never school him for so long that he becomes tired and bored with his exercises.

Hacking is good all-round exercise, giving the horse zest while providing some relaxation from the more formal schooling, though helping his balance with a rider, especially in gentle work up and down hills.

The four-year-old should hack out three or four days a week for up to one hour at the most, while being schooled two or three times a week. Formal lessons at home should last for up to half an hour each, but not more; in this way no excess strain will be put upon him.

SUMMARY of beginning stages of training the four-year-old:

First week—This is a refresher period, reminding the young horse to accept and carry the weight of a rider. Remember that throughout this training the young horse should be turned out for at least one hour each day.

1st day—Fit boots, snaffle bridle, lungeing cavesson and roller, and side reins. Lunge the horse on a circle of forty feet diameter for twenty minutes, changing direction frequently, with side reins fitted so that when the horse lowers his head he makes contact with them. As training progresses the side reins may be shortened gradually.

2nd day—Repeat yesterday's lesson, lungeing the horse, but this time with saddle fitted. After the horse has worked for twenty minutes, a lightweight rider may lie across his back in preparation for backing. Although these lessons were given last year it is still important for them to be repeated before passing on to the next stages.

49

Trotting over ground rails

3rd day—Lunge the horse as previously for about fifteen minutes, then a rider may mount and ride the horse on the lunge for ten minutes.

4th day—The horse is first lunged without a rider, then with rider in the saddle for not more than twenty minutes.

5th and 6th days—The horse is first worked on the lunge without the rider then with the rider, in all for about twenty minutes. He can then be hacked around the field or *manège* for half an hour.

7th day—Rest day for horse, trainer and rider. Turn horse out into the field for two or more hours.

Second week

1st day—All exercises of first week should have caused little difficulty, having been learned the previous year. Today the horse should be mounted and lunged and then ridden in the *manège* for about half an hour.

2nd day—Lunge the horse first and then hack out, again with that older horse, for about three-quarters of an hour.

3rd day—Lunge work for ten minutes, then hacking exercise, including work on slopes.

4th day—Lunge work for ten minutes and then work the horse on large circles, loops and serpentines, working in the *manège* for about twenty minutes.

5th day—Hack out for one hour.

6th day—Schooling—lunge the horse over ground rails and then ride him over them. Work on transitions and changes of direction (see examples on page 47. Diagrams 1-12).

7th day—Rest for all—as before. Do not forget to turn him out into the field.

Third week—By now the horse should be in improved condition. Make any necessary adjustments to his diet by increasing the concentrates and cutting down the bulk if he is lazy.

1st day—Lunge the horse for twenty minutes—he may be fresh after his rest-day. With all your lunge work use as large a circle as possible, encouraging the horse to go freely forwards. After lungeing, the horse should be ridden for thirty minutes, and encouraged to respond to leg aids.

2nd day—Hack out with an older horse with the object of introducing the trainee to light traffic. Try to arrange the ride after the horse has been ridden about the field for half an hour in the company of your experienced horse. This should last an hour.

3rd day—Again hack out—and now introduce your horse to cantering up gentle slopes in straight lines.

4th day—Work on long reins—this exercise develops your horse's mobility and obedience to orders. Ride him for half an hour 'at home', working on circles, loops, serpentines, transitions and over ground rails.

5th day—Take the horse out for a cross-country ride for about one and a half hours to see that he cultivates balance with his rider by working over uneven, undulating ground.

6th day—Work at lungeing over ground rails and then ride for half an hour.

7th day—Rest. Turn out for two or more hours.

Fourth week

1st day—Lunge the horse for ten minutes as usual after his rest-day to work out his freshness. Ride him for twenty minutes only, on turns and circles and then transitions.

2nd day—Hack out—as usual with that older horse, and continue familiarising the trainee horse with light traffic.

3rd day—Work on the lunge with the object of loosening the horse's back and improving his suppleness. Progress to ground rails and finally to a small spread fence eighteen inches high and eighteen inches wide. The jump should be twice the distance away from the last pole as the distance between the poles. If your poles are four feet six inches apart the fence will be nine feet away from your last pole.

4th day—Work in a large field, preferably on a hill, or else go for a cross-country hack.

5th day—Lunge for twenty minutes making changes of pace and transitions. The side reins may now be fitted so that there is contact, the horse always being asked to seek a contact and look for the rein. Work for a further forty minutes by hacking out to allow the horse to relax.

6th day—Work in the *manège* with the rider up for ten minutes at limbering-up exercises, making large loops, serpentines, circles and changes of direction. This loosens the horse's back and allows him to settle down to work easily. Progress to ground rails and small gymnastic jumping exercises, that is, ground rails at four feet six inches apart to a small fence nine to ten feet from the last rail (see example opposite). This will allow the horse to stretch his neck, looking down to the ground with a rounded body outline; this helps to develop the pushing power from his hind legs.

7th day—Rest the horse and turn out as usual into the field for two or more hours. Turning the horse out in the field for rest and relaxation daily throughout his training will help to prevent boredom and restlessness.

8. Improving the horse's agility by loose schooling

If you have followed my programme, your young horse should now be fit and ready for jumping lessons. 'Loose schooling' is, oddly enough, carried out in an enclosed space—in a well-fenced *manège* or indoor school. The school should be no larger than about one hundred feet by fifty feet. If a school is larger than that it will be more difficult for the trainer to keep control over the trainee horse. The trainer positions himself and moves in such a way that he keeps the horse moving in the direction of his choice and at a controlled speed. Keeping opposite the horse's shoulder, and holding the whip pointing towards the shoulder, he keeps the horse out to the school wall, or, by moving to be opposite the horse's quarters, with the whip towards the quarters, maintains impulsion and speed.

It is important to stress at this stage that the horse must not be hustled. This will only disconcert him. He must learn to respond, as before, to the voice and go forward calmly with that confidence he should by now have gained in his trainer. If he is fussed or frightened by his trainer he will try to gallop and leap about, and in this way he will lose confidence and perhaps even injure himself.

Loose jumping helps to strengthen the necessary muscles and encourages him to use his head and neck while allowing him to round his back and fold his legs when negotiating a jump. He must loose school calmly and obediently on the flat before attempting loose jumping.

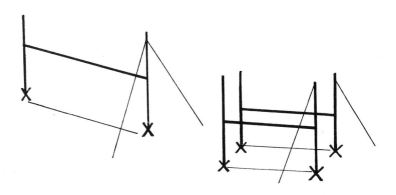

A good arrangement for loose schooling over jumps is as follows: put a single rail on two uprights at approximately one foot from the ground at right angles to the wall of the school with a ground rail and a sloping rail set as a wing, to discourage the horse from running out. When he is jumping well over this, progress to a fence of approximately two feet high and two feet wide.

As soon as the horse is jumping confidently while schooled loose he is ready to begin his mounted jumping training. I believe that the best results are achieved with a four-year-old if he is subjected to a progressive training programme for the first eight months of his fourth year. This should comprise work on the flat and over fences, with one complementing the other—the jumping giving the horse bounce and impulsion and keeping his body fit and his mind alert; the flat work, or dressage training, making him immediately responsive to natural aids. This combined training should produce a useful, well-mannered horse with the ability to work as well on the flat as over jumps.

Begin your mounted jumping exercises by walking the horse over poles lying on the ground; these should be spaced out evenly, at about four to five feet apart. As his confidence appears to increase, he can be worked at the trot, keeping the rails at the same distance apart. The rails should now be arranged differently, on a straight course, in a circle, and also made to form a corner, making sure that the distances between the middle of the poles is the same, and the horse should now work over them making various changes of direction.

Used thus, the rails develop the horse's thrust from his hind legs. It should not be long before the youngster is working over the ground rails calmly and confidently on both reins. Progressing from this work on ground rails, the horse may now be encouraged to jump a small fence. Keep the distance of the four feet six inches as between the ground rails but this time only use three poles and place a small fence one foot high nine feet away from the last rail (see diagram on page 52).

The horse must be ridden boldly and firmly at the trot with energy and rhythm while the rider looks forward beyond the fence. The horse should trot confidently through the first three ground rails, maintaining a regular pace, and should jump the small fence easily.

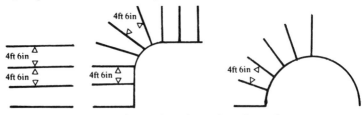

Rearrange the exercise and work on the other rein.

Practise on both reins, sometimes over the obstacles, sometimes riding in the cleared space of the *manège*, so that balance and rhythm is maintained throughout. Your trainee should now be obeying your aids confidently without rushing his fences. Progress through all phases of the schooling should be gradual.

As previously advised, you should hack out across country for about an hour and a half, three days a week. On other days the horse should have his schooling on the flat and over jumps. Once a week it is a good idea to rest the horse's back and lunge him. In brief your programme could be:

Monday—Hack out, across country
Tuesday—Flat work
Wednesday—Road work
Thursday—Ground rails and some jumping
Friday—Flat work
Saturday—Hack out, hill work
Sunday—Lunge

By now your horse should be able to canter safely when hacking on a straight course and up and down gentle slopes. If so, and if he is also confident in the trot over ground rails, he is ready to begin training at the canter in the *manège*. One of the best ways to develop and improve the horse's canter stride is to place three poles on the ground twenty feet apart. The horse, cantering in the *manège*, maintains a canter over the poles taking each pole in a canter stride, with a canter stride between each one.

The working canter on a long rein

Riding across country at all paces to develop balance

Starting position for the turn on the forehand

Turn on the forehand: the quarters move round the horse's pivoting forehand

Turn on the forehand: the near hind moves across the off hind

Shoulder-in progressing out of the corner

Hill work is another excellent method of developing self-balance

Lungeing over a small fence. Notice the rails which prevent the lunge line getting hooked up

Gymnastic work may next be introduced by replacing those ground rails with three small jumps at a distance of twenty feet apart. Enter this exercise in a controlled, balanced canter but gaining extra momentum as the horse goes through the grid. You should alternate this with the exercises at trot until your horse is confident in his gymnastic jumping from the trot *or* the canter at the demands of his rider. In your efforts to improve the horse's jumping ability, do not forget to continue developing basic dressage.

Developing balance and judgement of stride
Work over combination fences is one of the ways to develop the young horse's judgement of stride, with agility and proper balance over and between fences. It is not necessary at this stage to practise over very large obstacles—work progressively by using various low combination fences. Remember that it is preferable to increase the spread—the width—of a fence rather than its height, because the horse will be encouraged to jump smoothly and in good style.

Such simple gymnastic jumping develops your horse's confidence—indeed it has the same effect on a more experienced horse which has been trained incorrectly or has lost his confidence through a fall or because he has been overfaced i.e. been asked to jump over bigger, more difficult fences than he could cope with at the time.

In the arrangement of combination fences for schooling the horse, it must be remembered that an upright fence will encourage him to lift his shoulders, particularly if he is what is known as a short striding horse, while spread fences encourage the horse to stretch out and slightly arch, or round, his back. Careful planning of fences for the trot and canter exercises, using uprights and spreads, will develop the horse's jumping skill and teach him to use himself correctly.

Here is a simple lay-out for a gymnastic exercise—

Arrange a ground rail twenty feet from a small upright fence about two feet six inches high. Place another pole twenty feet from the upright. After the second ground rail, make a small spread fence two feet six inches high by three feet wide about twenty-one feet away. (See diagram on page 62).

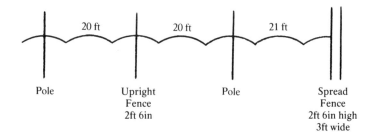

	20 ft		20 ft		21 ft	
Pole		Upright Fence 2ft 6in		Pole		Spread Fence 2ft 6in high 3ft wide

This exercise will help the horse to canter in good style. The little upright at a short distance of twenty feet, will help the horse to lighten his forehand and jump accurately with energy and pushing power from his hindquarters. The pole will again correct the canter stride and ensure that the horse meets the spread fence properly and jumps it with a rounded back.

Certain horses tend to be impetuous and will rush their fences because they find jumping exciting, and for this type of horse I have found that ground rails on the circle will help to balance the horse and prevent him from rushing. Work with rails four feet six inches apart (at rail centre) on a circle of sixty feet in diameter. When carrying out such schooling as I have described here, have ground rails in one part of the *manège* and jumps in another part. This enables you to vary the exercises—working over the fences and then going over the ground rails—checking that the horse is still maintaining rhythm in his paces. Those horses which become excited when jumping should be settled by riding around the fences and then over the ground rails before tackling the jumping exercise.

Footnote
The benefits of various types of fences, with relative distances and proportions, are outlined in *Jumping Explained*.

9. Developing a four-year-old's courage and initiative

This is best done by riding him to hounds. Before the young horse is taken hunting he should be absolutely obedient to the rider and established in the basic training described so far. There will then be no risk of spoiling his mouth by the rider resorting to pulling on the reins when the young horse becomes excited.

Cub-hunting begins in September, and foxhunting proper in November, continuing until February or March depending on weather and land conditions. On average the young horse may be taken once a fortnight for up to two hours throughout the season. Hunting your young horse helps to develop self-reliance, initiative, confidence and courage. Even when a horse has not had a long day's hunting or had to go very fast, he will still be tired from the mental and physical exercise he has experienced and should rest after every day's hunting, just being led out in hand for half an hour. Hunting is an excellent introduction to all cross-country work but your horse must be made fit for this extra activity. In all but the most simple preparations for his hunting, use that more experienced horse as his companion and pace-maker. Begin with walking exercises progressing to slow trotting. Roadwork may be introduced between four and six weeks before hunting begins using a minimum of work up and down hills at first, then gradually taking the horse on to steeper inclines. Assuming that he displays fitness in all this, he is ready to begin cross-country schooling.

The horse must be able to shorten and lengthen his canter stride obediently and move smoothly between the rider's leg and hand. Practise jumping small solid fences from the trot and canter — he must be able to jump from the slower pace as well as from the faster pace. School the youngster over a course containing well-built, solid-looking fences with the older horse taking the lead.

Ditches can be disconcerting to the inexperienced horse, so be sure to jump your horse over small ones at first, with the older horse making the pace and setting the example. It is best to jump banks with a young horse from the trot, making it easier for him to maintain balance with thrust. Water jumps will, invariably, cause problems, therefore make certain that the bed of any water-jump is sound before using it. It is natural for the youngster to be somewhat nervous of jumping when encountering water and here again he should be given a lead by an experienced and reliable horse. If you have led your young horse through puddles and water as part of his early training, problems will now be minimal, though one must always face the possibility that a horse which has been taught to go through water may not recognise a water jump as such.

Jumping a small spread fence

10. Further exercises and movements

The turn on the forehand is one of the first movements that the young horse must master before he is able to give the best response to a rider's leg aids. From the halt, in a turn to the right on the forehand, the rider uses right rein and right leg. The rider's left rein and left leg balance and support. The horse must be ridden firmly into a well-balanced halt. The rider uses the right leg, vibrating a little to the rear of the girth, with the right rein maintaining bend so that the horse moves his hindquarters away from the right leg, while the left leg, at the girth, has the effect of preventing the horse from stepping back. The left rein controls the turn and helps to prevent the horse from walking forwards. The horse should step neither backwards nor forwards but it is considered a lesser fault if he steps forwards. The young horse must be ridden firmly forwards after completing the turn. This movement, once mastered, is best not practised too often because the horse will begin to anticipate. (See pages 58-9).

Turning on the forehand not only teaches the horse to respond more positively to a rider's aids but gives the latter control of the quarters and this is useful when out hunting or on cross-country rides for opening—and, if necessary, *closing*—gates.

Shoulder-in—this is a movement in which the horse is bent round the rider's inside leg (in shoulder-in right, the rider's right leg), with the horse's body bent away from the direction in which he is moving. The horse must maintain the rhythm of the pace, walk or trot, moving forwards and sideways with regular steps. It is a movement not to be attempted without an experienced person to help you. The aids are: the inside leg at the girth, indicating to the horse to move forwards and sideways, maintaining energy; the outside leg behind the girth, controlling the hindquarters; the inside rein indicates the bend to the inside while the outside rein controls the speed of the movement. It is best to begin the movement by riding a circle and riding shoulder-in from a tangent to the circle. With a young horse always ride a circle or go away on a diagonal line when the shoulder-in steps are completed.

Gymnastic work

Work over ground rails helps to develop calmness and, in conjunction with work over small fences, the horse's natural jumping ability will be improved. The ground rail will encourage the horse to elevate his body, thus developing greater power from behind. They will also help the horse's strength and stamina. The distance between rails must be correct, and should be adjusted for the various horses working over them. I have listed the distances below:

At a trot—Distance between each ground rail: four feet six inches. *At a trot*—Distance between the rails and small jump: nine feet. Distances may have to be varied slightly, according to the length of stride of individual horses.

11. New experiences for the four-year-old

Travelling

The procedure for preparing a foal or yearling to travel has already been described, but you may not have owned your horse from his early days. You may have bought him as a four-year-old and so I have outlined some pointers to observe when loading and transporting a new, and perhaps difficult, young horse.

1 Position the horse-box or trailer alongside a hedge or in the entrance to a gateway, where natural wings will be formed. Place the ramp level by resting on an incline so that the ramp is less steep than if placed on level ground.
2 Have his feed and haynet ready and open the front ramp of the trailer to get maximum light inside—the trailer itself having been placed, as for the very young horse, in such a way as to get maximum light to the interior of the box. You will of course need an assistant who should carry a lungeing rein.
3 Put a headcollar on the horse with a bridle over it. Dress the horse for travelling with tail bandage, tailguard, stable bandages, knee boots, rug, roller, over-reach boots and poll guard.
4 Walk the horse as straight as possible to the box, do not hesitate but do not rush him. Try to stay close to his shoulder without either looking back or getting in front of him.
5 Having walked your horse right inside the box, have your assistant attach the rear strap quickly so that the horse does not attempt to reverse out again. Tie up—removing the bridle which you put over the headcollar. Allow the horse sufficient rope so that he can eat his hay but not enough to allow him to turn around and perhaps bite the second horse if two are travelling together.

If your newly acquired horse has previously experienced bad travelling or unsympathetic handling when being loaded, he may be nervous and the following hints may prove useful in overcoming this.

A nervous horse, which will not even look at a box, let alone approach it, presents a problem. You must allow plenty of time to accomplish the job—never try to load any horse in a hurry, much less the nervous type; you will only increase his fears. Encourage him with a feed, handle him firmly, quietly and kindly. If he is used to long-reining you may be able to fit long reins and drive him in—but long-reining a nervous horse which is not accustomed to the exercise could cause him to panic and prevent you from loading him altogether. If, however, he can be controlled by you at his head while on a long rein used by an assistant who will be prompt in adjusting the back-strap, you may have good results. Do not attempt this unless you have an expert to help you.

Another problem could be presented by the horse which stands at the edge of the ramp and will go no further, swinging his quarters and always retreating away from the ramp. Get this horse as far as the edge of the ramp, standing quietly, take a lungeing line, fix one end firmly to the trailer, pass the line behind him, placing it just above the hocks and then go forwards into the box. Sometimes loading another, tractable and easy-going horse first, will induce the nervous horse to follow. There are other things one can do to help but it is best for you to ask for advice from someone experienced in loading difficult horses.

It is sensible to load difficult horses regularly, even when no journey is contemplated; simply get them into the box and feed them there while the box is stationary, so that they begin to think of the box as another stable.

When actually on the move, the driver must give the horse as comfortable a ride as possible, using all gears and changing up and down frequently, driving slowly, especially on bends and corners, so that he avoids giving the horse valid reasons for being afraid of entering into and travelling quietly in the trailer in future.

Shoeing

As a general rule the feet of your horse should be seen by a farrier at least once a month to check that they do not become too long.

It will be necessary for a young horse to be shod as soon as he begins regular schooling work, as otherwise his feet will wear down more quickly than the horn grows, causing soreness. If the horse has had regular visits from the farrier since it was a foal, just having his feet picked up experimentally and his hooves occasionally rasped, he will be confident when handled by the farrier. On the first occasion of having a young horse shod, I ask for lightweight front shoes only to be fitted, so that the youngster does not have to stand for too long while the farrier works. I leave it until the next time he needs shoes to have him shod all round. If he is stabled where other horses are kept, then I suggest you ask the farrier to pick up the youngster's feet whenever he comes to the stables. Most farriers are prepared to oblige in this since they know that it is important in the training of a young horse that he becomes easy in a farrier's presence and gains the necessary confidence about being shod in the future.

The use of studs
Studs can be fitted by the farrier or screwed in by yourself when you need them as long as you have asked the farrier to put stud holes in the outside heels of the shoes when he makes them. Studs give the horse security on difficult ground as they are anti-slip—various types are manufactured for use when riding on varying ground conditions and for different purposes.
None of these will be necessary, however, until the horse is well into his fourth year. They are used to give the horse grip, and thus confidence for jumping, and to enable the horse to progress at all paces up to and including full gallop over all kinds of terrain. If the ground proves very heavy and muddy, all shoes should have screw-holes, and large, square studs be used. If, on the other hand, the ground has been made slippery through a heavy shower of rain, pointed studs on all four feet should be employed. If the ground is considered perfect, with some spring in it, use small studs for work outside on the flat or in a dressage phase of a competition, also when showing in riding-horse or equitation classes. For show-jumping I prefer the large, dome-shaped studs on each shoe, while for cross-country riding I use similar studs but in the hind shoes only.

Clipping
If your horse is stable kept and working hard during the winter

he will need to be clipped, but this should be undertaken by an experienced person so that your young horse is not frightened. Clipping is by no means done for appearances only—a heavy coat of hair has the same effect on a horse as working him while he is wearing a heavy rug. The horse with a well-clipped, short coat dries off quickly after working and is therefore less vulnerable to chills and, of course, it is easier for you to keep him clean and well-groomed. The horse is naturally provided with a layer of protective fat beneath his skin and this goes a long way in keeping out the cold, but the clipped horse must be provided with adequate clothing as a substitute for his natural coat. Both the operation of clipping and the wearing of substitute clothing are, in themselves, new lessons for the young horse to learn.

These are brief remarks on the subject, giving the fundamental reasons for clipping.If you, as owner-trainer of your own horse, want to undertake the task of clipping your horse you should take advice on the equipment needed and the approach you must make to the work. Do not clip a young horse for the first time until you have had considerable experience clipping older horses.

Careful trimming will improve the appearance of the horse. The hairs of mane and tail will pluck easily when pores of the skin are open, that is, during warm weather or after exercise. The mane is pulled to thin it out, to reduce a long mane to a shorter length or to get it to lie flat. The longest hairs should be plucked first from underneath and removed, a few at a time, by winding them around a finger or a mane comb. When trimming it is again best to have an assistant to hold the horse so that he is comforted and does not fidget. The whole mane need not be completed at one time.

The tail is pulled to improve shape and appearance. Tail pulling is again done by plucking out the hairs, beginning at the top of the tail from the underneath and working one's way down the tail until a good shape is achieved. Again it is imperative to seek expert advice before attempting to trim a horse on your own.

Plaiting the mane

This is done to show off the neck and head and will be

necessary for your riding-horse or equitation class in shows. If the horse has a well-shaped head and neck then small tight plaits will enhance its appearance even more. If, however, the neck is straight and badly shaped it can be improved by careful and clever plaiting. The mane can be plaited to give an illusion of greater breadth in the neck if you brush the mane over on the nearside and spray the top hair half way down with lacquer, and then brush over to the offside, plait and roll into neat knobs. Sometimes the horse becomes excited when his mane is being plaited so it is better to do this on the morning of a competition or meet, always being sure to follow your usual routine as far as possible. If you are able to watch an expert before attempting to plait a mane yourself, you will soon learn how to do it.

The first horse show

This is a good preparation for getting your horse to work in the company of other, strange, horses, an occasion for getting him accustomed to sights and sounds which he may not experience in his everyday life at home.

Naturally this should be a dress rehearsal in the truest sense—he will need to be equipped with everything normally needed on a journey to a show—a headcollar, rope, grooming kit, summer sheet and anti-sweat rug, in case his experiences over-excite and over-heat him, while tail-bandage, tailguard, knee pads, stable bandages and poll guard (made of foam rubber sewn onto the headcollar so that if he should throw up his head while in the trailer he will not damage himself), must be worn to protect him when travelling to and from the show. Take his haynet and water bucket, and also a container of water, and do not forget first-aid equipment for horse and rider, and his lungeing equipment. Your tack must, of course, be clean and in good order—check all stitching for safety. Take the horse's lunch-time hard feed so that his usual dietary routine is disturbed as little as possible.

In all aspects of making the journey for your horse's introduction to the show atmosphere, preparing him in the stable and loading him, leave yourself plenty of time. The best results will be achieved if you are not in any hurry. This rehearsal for the real thing can take the form of several visits to shows without actually entering him in any class—simply take him to the show grounds to ride him around letting him become used to the atmosphere. On your arrival do not unload him immediately. Look him over to make certain that he has travelled well and suffered no ill-effects from his journey, then set about finding your own bearings—locate the conveniences, the collecting and main rings and decide where it is safest to ride him about. When you do ride him around you will need as much space as you can get for any manoeuvres you may have to make.

Before unloading your horse remove all his travelling equipment. Fit his brushing boots and over-reach boots if the latter were not used when travelling. His saddle and bridle should also be fitted while he is in the box. Next fit his lungeing cavesson over the bridle. You should yourself be wearing a hard hat and gloves. Now that you are ready for the unloading, get your assistant to unfasten the front ramp so that your horse can be led out—he may be hesitant, may stop and whinny, but this is quite usual—even so, be alert yourself for anything in the immediate vicinity which may startle him in this unfamiliar place. As soon as he is unloaded lead him to a space which you have previously picked out to put him onto a lunge circle, so that he has a chance to settle and relax after his journey. I usually lunge a young horse for as much as half an hour before mounting up. When you do mount your horse get your assistant to steady him and help you. Although you will manage this easily by yourself at home, in these strange surroundings it may be more difficult—your horse may still be restive and may even try to break away from you. Nothing is so embarrassing as to be afoot searching for a loose horse at a show just because you were not prepared and did not get this assistance. Once mounted, hack around the show ground, over a pre-planned route, quietly allowing your horse to see all the new sights and hear the unfamiliar sounds.

If you hack in this way for as long as an hour, your horse will be tired as, in all, he will have had an hour and a half exercising in this unfamiliar place. Now prepare him for his journey home. Firstly, remove his saddle and bridle, put on his headcollar with the poll guard attached; remove his brushing boots, put on his sheet and roller, bandages, knee pads and tail bandage; leave on his over-reach boots. Now he is ready to load into the trailer. Offer him a drink and then load him. You may again need the lunge line and your assistant should help you on the first two or three occasions of making such 'dummy runs' to show grounds, because the youngster will be more excited than usual. If such travelling lessons are well taught and fully learnt, your horse will come, in time, to be loaded without undue difficulty. Once he is in his box, give him his lunch-time feed, tie up his haynet and then allow him to stand in the stationary trailer for a short time before you start for home. Drive home as carefully as before so that the youngster's confidence is increased all the more for the next occasion.

The best competition in which to enter a young horse to gain experience is some type of showing class—either an equitation or riding-horse class where he will only be expected to show himself at walk, trot and canter on both reins. In these initial showings make sure that you do not get yourself boxed in by other riders crowding you behind, in front or to your sides, so that your horse has no space in which to manoeuvre. He may be excited, even want to buck and frisk about; you must ensure that he is not crowded as you ride him as calmly and firmly as you would in any exercises at home. Make this an enjoyable occasion for him.

In the riding-horse class your horse will be ridden, at one stage, by the judge. If you are not absolutely certain that his paces will be shown to their best advantage if he is ridden by someone other than yourself, it is best to withdraw from the competition before that stage is reached, simply by saying you are riding a young horse on his first outing in public.

In equitation classes it is unusual for anyone else but you, the owner-rider, to ride your horse so this is a most appropriate class in which to enter him initially. If you have an attractive, well-trained horse and feel it likely that you will be in the final front line, be prepared. Plan beforehand to work your horse in some simple manoeuvres—a 'routine' which will show him off well on both reins. I usually trot a large figure of eight, go into the canter for another figure of eight, making a change of leg by passing through trot and then coming out of the eight to lengthen the stride around the edge of the arena, returning to trot, walk and halt in front of the judges. Demonstrate your own calmness by being polite enough to thank the judges and smile.

The first dressage test

When your horse is trained in his basic paces and going forwards obediently, much useful experience can be gained for both his trainer and himself by taking part in a small competition. Follow your routine as closely as possible on the day before the competition so as not to disconcert the horse with unusual activities. Clean and check tack for safety—inspect all stitching in leather pieces, ensure that buckles and girth are sound. Your equipment will be the same as for any journey. The bridle to use here, however, is the snaffle.

On arrival at the dressage meeting check to ensure that the horse has travelled well and safely. Locate the secretary's tent to declare your intention to ride and collect your number. Find out which arena you are to ride in and whether the competition is running to schedule or whether it is behind time. With this information you will know how long you will have to 'ride your horse in', to settle him down after his journey. Do always allow yourself plenty of time so that at no point leading up to the competition are you rushed or flustered by any last minute hitch.

The 'riding in' period is very important. Ride in a relaxed manner, working the horse so that he becomes attentive. The time you allow for this depends on the temperament of your horse. If he appears to settle down in the atmosphere of the show ground, allow about half an hour's work. If, however, he is the excitable type, he may require as much as an hour and a half to 'ride in'. Try to keep calm yourself, even if the horse fusses, so that when you actually enter the arena you will be able to produce the best performance from your mount that he is capable of giving at this stage of his training. After your test, dismount, slacken the girth and make a fuss of your horse by feeding him some grass. Next, return him to his box, remove his tack and put on his headcollar. Give him a drink, put on his summer sheet and let him have his short feed.

Working the horse in a covered school

If you have been fortunate enough to gain easy access to an indoor school in which you have worked your youngster, he will have become quite accustomed to such indoor exercise from an early age. An indoor school is much the best place to back a young horse for the first time but some novices may not have been so lucky in that respect and will have carried out all early work in the open. There is no serious drawback in this—at least there has been no temptation to work on those tight circles and turns which can prove so detrimental to the youngster.

So many indoor schools are now being built that the dressage and show-jumping seasons appear to be running on throughout the year and it is advisable occasionally to hire an indoor school if there is one in your locality so that the horse will become used to going through his paces indoors as well as in the open. Some horses which have been consistently worked in the open will be nervous when brought to perform in an environment which is unfamiliar to them, and so they should have indoor work introduced to them from time to time before actually being tested in a competition set in an enclosed arena.

Show-jumping

This should not be undertaken until a horse is at least four and a half years old—approaching five.

Practise by riding over combination fences and then working over small courses, at home or at a riding club. Many riding clubs or pony club branches arrange schooling evenings when members are invited to attend and take their young horses to ride over a full set of show-jumps.

Choose a small competition for your horse's first jumping outing where you are confident that the fences are well-built and not over-large. Enter for one class only—even if your horse has done very well. Do not be tempted to enter several jumping classes and run the risk of your horse becoming 'over-faced'— set too high a standard and he may lose his nerve or begin to jump badly through boredom.

12. More experiences

It is quite all right to hunt the four-year-old provided he is in a really fit condition and is well-mannered. You should, however, take several precautions which are anyway dictated by good manners. Do not arrive at the meet too early, and when you do arrive, keep your young horse on the outskirts of the gathering of horses and hounds. If you take him, new to the meet, right into the middle, he will become excited and possibly unmanageable.

Keep your horse out of the way of others—riders, hunt-servants and hounds. Keep his head toward the hounds. This is only fair to him. With his quarters to the hounds milling about behind him, he may become unnerved and kick out. Hounds will pass behind other horses which are used to

Hunting — make sure your horse stands quietly at the meet

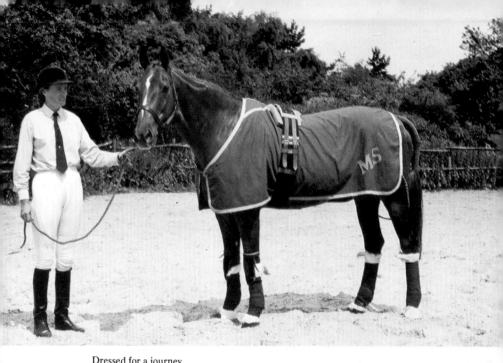

Dressed for a journey

Loading into a trailer

Jumping a small fence from trot

Developing athletic ability by small combination fences

An inviting spread fence; the pole on the ground helps the horse to judge his take-off

Riding a circle, the horse correctly bent

them—they are not to know that he is *not* used to them. On the first occasion do not keep him out for much more than an hour. If you do he may become too excited and over-tired.

On the first three or four occasions you will be trying to teach him his hunt manners—getting him used to the presence of many other horses and hounds without being tempted to kick out at anyone, and teaching him to remain calm and to allow other horses to overtake him in the field without him trying to throw you and then get out in front. It is usually the third or fourth outing which proves difficult. Young horses at their first two or three meets are pleasantly surprised and fascinated by the new sights, sounds and movements and thus they behave reasonably well. On that third or fourth time out, however, the youngster is beginning to see what it's all about and is gaining the spirit of the thing; he begins to anticipate each move and will become more excited, perhaps give trouble. It is now that you must assert yourself and ride him with firmness and calm, perhaps keeping him further away from other horses and the hounds than hitherto. After his first half-dozen meets you should find that your horse has settled down to enjoy with you a good season in the field.

13. Some health problems

The following are some disorders from which a young horse can suffer. In certain instances I have mentioned my own treatment, but as a novice-trainer without experience, you should seek the advice of the veterinary surgeon at any time if your horse shows those symptoms I have described here. Some of the disorders may occur in a horse which you have only recently acquired; perhaps nothing which has happened to the horse while with you has been the cause. If indeed you have not had your horse from an early age, it is as well for you to know what to look for after his arrival.

Sweating

A horse may be found to break out in a heavy sweat some time after being brought into the stable after working and dried off thoroughly. This excessive sweating is the result of nerves — it is a nervous reaction to work which the horse has found exciting. Try to bring the horse in as calmly as possible, going so far as to dismount and walk for the last half mile home if you have been working across country. After leading in, give him his haynet, make sure that he is dry and warm, and return later to ascertain whether he is in fact settling down. The excessive sweating usually occurs on neck, flank and behind the ears. It may help to use a nylon girth on such a horse to allow more air to get to the skin in this area where sweating is likely to occur. If you do dismount and walk your horse in from half a mile, or even a mile away from home, loosen the girth.

Weaving

This name is given to another nervous disorder — although really it is a habit, and it is 'catching' in that one horse will imitate another which is subject to it. It causes the horse, while stationary, to swing its head from side to side while the front legs are set apart. Although weaving is usually a manifestation of boredom it can actually be inherited and sometimes a young horse will weave if kept in the company of another 'weaver'. Try to relieve any boredom by varying exercise periods and alternate by turning the horse out to grass. If you follow those programmes for training which I have already set down, never leaving your horse too long to his own devices, you should not have a bored horse which may become subject to this.

Crib-biting

This is seen when a horse grips an object, such as the top of a stable half-door, biting on it and sucking in air at the same time. It may be compared to the human habit of biting nails or chewing on a pencil end and is another symptom of boredom. In the first instance try to remove any object on which the horse tends to bite. I have sometimes found that brushing the top edge of a stable half-door with creosote discourages a horse from gripping and chewing at it but, of course, the real cure is to relieve his boredom. Vary your horse's work as much as possible. Split up the training periods in such a way that the strict routine is broken — instead of one longish session work for two shorter sessions and turn your horse out into the field for a part of the day, weather and all else permitting, so that he is not just standing in his stable with nothing to do.

Wind-sucking

This is another nervous habit.The horse appears to draw in air more deeply and frequently than is normal. The same applies here as to weaving and crib-biting — vary his working life as much as possible.

Worms

Since this is not a textbook about the ills of horses I will only briefly deal with some of the symptoms and treatment of and for worms. In all suspected cases of worms it is a matter for professional veterinary treatment. A horse should be wormed regularly, i.e. every six to eight weeks, with one of the modern drugs available from a veterinary surgeon or pharmacist. If they are present in his system because of poor grazing it is best to seek some advice from the vet on how to improve the pasture.

Redworm

Unfortunately this is common in young horses and is a result of grazing in a field which is, colloquially, 'horse sick' — infected pasture. The horse appears to eat well enough but still loses flesh, has a dry, dull coat, is dull-eyed and subject to diarrhoea. Horses with redworm are sometimes also anaemic. Call in the veterinary surgeon for advice about diet and treatment. Sometimes worms can be detected in the horse's droppings — by a special process, the vet examines the dung and makes a fairly accurate assessment of the degree of infestation of these and other worms.

Bot-worm

Known in equestrian circles as 'stomach bot', here the bot-fly is the villain. The horse appears to have a good appetite but does not seem to benefit by it since he will have weight-loss, and a dull or 'staring' coat. Stomach bot is a parasite produced by the bot-fly in pastures where a horse may graze. As the horse is grazing, the fly lays its eggs on his legs and in licking them the horse absorbs them into his intestines where the maggot finally hatches out. The eggs, which are very small and yellow, may appear on the horse's legs during the spring and summer months. They can be clipped away and, on the vet's advice, a powder can be administered to the horse. Treat on professional advice.

Round-worm

The symptoms are few, but a horse suffering from this parasite may have attacks of colic, which you may detect from his general restlessness, lying down and getting up, looking round at his flanks or kicking at his belly. These symptoms are usually accompanied by irregular bowel movement. Call in your veterinary surgeon for advice on diet and treatment. The causes are again poor pasture and failure to remove dropping on a weekly basis.

Whip-worm

This worm appears at the rectum of the horse. The general symptoms are a yellow discharge under the root of the tail, and the horse will rub his tail on the wall or manger. Veterinary advice should be sought. Poor, stale grazing produces the conditions in which a horse contracts this, and here again advice should be sought.

It is important to inspect your horse regularly, to watch out for any odd habit which he may develop and ensure that his eye remains bright and coat in good condition. If in doubt always seek professional veterinary advice.

Fencing must be sound and adequate for the size of the horse ▶

14. Other problems

Stable manners

If you have only recently acquired a horse and he is therefore strange to your stables and perhaps has not had that early training which, as I have described, a young horse should receive from a very early age, you may find that his general behaviour is bad. Initially he must be taught obedience in the simplest things: to be tied up without fuss, to move over in the stable, and to allow his feet to be picked up and inspected.

Start from the beginning — tying him up, using a strong leather headcollar which should fit well and stand up to the strain of any fidgeting on his part. Attach a length of string to the tie-up ring so that should he pull back while alone in the stable, he will break the string — not his headcollar. The string should be secured with a slip-knot for quick release. Give your horse a net of hay to keep him occupied and lightly groom him for about ten minutes. If during all this he appears to be settling in calmly, untie him and leave him in his stable. Follow the same procedure on your next visit, again tying him up. Try picking up his feet, holding up the leg for a moment or two, then let it down and pat him. Do the same with each leg in turn, always with that comforting pat. Groom again and leave him. On no account should a young horse simply be taken into a new stable, tied up and then left alone. With such abrupt treatment he may well become nervous, take fright, pull back and perhaps injure himself. Although almost all of the foregoing has been remarked on in previous pages, I have been referring to the early training of a very young horse accustomed to correct handling almost from birth—here we are dealing with a healthy youngster, fully grown but without all the advantages of that early training.

As mentioned earlier, the best method of teaching a horse to move over in the stable is to press your hand to his side with the word 'over' so that in time he associates the word with the pressure, and will eventually act on either voice or touch.

Initial training such as this will be instilled by regular handling, two or three times a day, *every* day.

The new horse may be nervous of a farrier and prove difficult to shoe. I have found that this can be due to the fact that in his very young days he may have been accustomed only to women and girls around his stable. The appearance of a man meant discomfort of some sort, the man having been a veterinary surgeon, called in to give him some sort of treatment which he associated with discomfort or in some cases even pain, through some injury he had sustained. It is a fact that there is always a larger number of girls than men or boys regularly employed around riding stables or as volunteer workers, whom the horse associates with kindly treatment and comfortable routine. Apart from persuading any male visitors to come and pat your horse and speak to him in your stable — perhaps even help with his grooming and, if you trust their horsemanship, to ride him — ask any farrier who may be attending to other horses in the vicinity to pay an experimental visit to him. The farrier need only pick up your horse's feet and perhaps run his rasp around the hooves. A good blacksmith or farrier will be only too glad to oblige knowing this kind of familiarisation will save fuss and discomfort to all concerned at a later date. In all the foregoing I am assuming that my reader is a girl. Even so, the same applies if the owner of the newcomer to the stable is male.

If your new horse proves difficult to saddle this could be because he has had the saddle banged down on his back and the girth done up too tightly when he was young and therefore associates this with discomfort. The horse may be provided with a numnah to fit under the saddle and a nylon girth which may prove more comfortable for this type of horse to wear. Since he has shown reluctance to be girthed do this gradually; after saddling up with girth adjusted only reasonably firmly, let him stand in his stable for a while to get used to the feel of it after making sure that no part of his tack is pinching him anywhere, and that the girth buckles lie comfortably on the saddle flaps with buckle guards in position.

The girth strap should have a few spare holes on each side for future adjustments. When the horse is brought from his stable and the girth made safe, mount from a mounting block, and after riding quietly for five or ten minutes, tighten the girth if necessary. Patient handling always pays dividends.

I will here deal with some of the problems which may present themselves to the owner-trainer of a newly acquired four-year-old when he is taken from his stable to be ridden. He may shy for no reason apparent to his rider and at unexpected moments in his initial outings. It is always wise to be accompanied by a rider on an older, more experienced horse which is accustomed to all the local sights, sounds and surroundings. This more mature horse will be a calming influence on the new 'boy' and the tendency to shy should cease. The rider should concentrate on riding the horse firmly forwards on a prescribed course. Do not attempt to chastise with a whip — this only confuses the young horse more and will in some cases actually frighten him and in his fear he will become even less easy to manage.

Horses have their individual characters and shying is sometimes a pose or can be due to freshness, playfulness or sheer mischievousness, a testing of *you* by the horse. If you feel that this is indeed the case you should continue to ride through the problem in ·a no-nonsense fashion, trying to ignore this behaviour. As your horse becomes accustomed to your patient, calm but firm training and is consequently better educated, you will be able to use shoulder-in, as explained on page 65, thus compelling the horse to continue forwards in response to your aids — going forwards 'from the leg' without any shying. A horse may shy at something which moves in a hedge, some piece of litter which flutters, during a cross-country ride or on the road, swinging his quarters away from the object. It is best here to use the aids for a turn on the forehand while still urging him forwards. If the horse shies at some object on your left, you should bring your right leg back to control his quarters and move the left while maintaining a flexible hold with the right rein. In this way your mount is discouraged from side-stepping into the path of a following horse or any road traffic.

Health problems apart, if the nature of your new horse makes him sluggish or lazy, it can be that he is a late developer. Be as patient with him as always, work him only lightly, seek advice on the best protein diet, give him regular exercise and all the care and attention already described. If you are prepared to follow this advice over a period of from four to six months, such treatment should turn a horse of indifferent behaviour into a well-mannered and obedient mount. Use the dressage whip to support your leg aids until he has learnt to answer to the lightest aid.

You may have a young horse which is what is called 'over-bent'. Briefly, this means that, when being ridden, the horse's head comes behind the vertical line with his muzzle tucked in towards his chest. I would suggest that you equip him with a jointed eggbutt snaffle, which is a mild bit. Using this type of snaffle, school the horse on the flat, without asking him to flex (bend). If he persists in over-bending, ride him forwards while keeping him on a fairly long rein. Lungeing can be used to encourage his free forward movement with increase and decrease of pace. At the same time you will be getting the horse to lengthen and shorten his stride to order. If this work on the flat and lungeing appears to be successful, go on to work over ground rails in such a way as to encourage him to take a longer stride on a long rein.

Since it has already been established that the horse's impulsion or thrust for jumping comes from his hindquarters, he must be trained to expect contact or 'look for' the rein—his energy, as it were, coming through the rider's hands.

Refusals — their cause and cure is a subject which could occupy the major part of a book. Here I have outlined some of the reasons for a horse's reluctance to take a jump. Confidence, or rather the lack of it, can be communicated to a horse by his rider in the same way as fear, and a horse may refuse a jump because he lacks confidence in his rider, who himself is not confident. A manifestation of this is a rider's tendency to apply too much pressure on the reins thus restricting the natural movement of the horse's head. Another reason for baulking on the horse's part is that a fence may be set at an awkward angle to his run for take-off. A horse which lacks balance will become heavy on his forehand, that is to say his front legs are pulling his body along rather than his hindlegs driving his body, so that he has difficulty in lifting himself off the ground.

A horse may appear stubborn and will refuse simply through careless and ill-advised early training when he was not taught to move forwards from the rider's aids. A horse which is otherwise well behaved may hesitate because the very hard ground is jarring his legs and he will come to a halt. It is inadvisable to jump a young horse when the ground is hard.

It should be obvious that an unfit horse will not give of his best.

Horse *and* rider should both be fit for what is a very exacting form of sport. A horse with the best intentions can be let down by the rider. Poor presentation by the rider of his horse to the fence is letting down the horse. The best horse will not do his best with a poor rider.

Although I have written for the novice trainer, it must be presumed, if a reader has ambitions as a show-jumper, that he or she is not a raw novice rider. It is an equestrian truism that a 'green' horse should not be trained by an equally inexperienced rider. In the first instance the rider should have trained on an experienced horse which is already a proficient jumper — in this circumstance the horse becoming a 'trainer' in his turn. The rider thus gains confidence and that confidence is conveyed to the novice-horse so that with its instinctive desire to obey and its natural courage, the horse will answer to what is a challenge to both him and his rider.

Another problem is presented by the horse which goes too fast at the trot and this is usually the result of lack of balance of both horse and rider. The rider must try to ride in such a way as to improve his or her own balance and rhythm while not interfering with the horse's movements. The rider should practise maintaining a secure and 'deep' seat by riding a well-trained, more mature horse without using stirrups — after a while working in large circles, loops and serpentines and using changes of pace. Work a fast-trotting horse on as light a rein as possible, stroking his neck to reassure and relax him. If the rider's own lessons on the older horse have been learnt and his or her own balance and seat are good, then the horse will improve his own balance. If the rider of a fast trotter adjusts his own rise and fall in the trot, this will have the effect of slowing down the horse's pace — thus between them harmony is achieved.

A young horse may tend to 'go under his fences' which, in the language of the show-grounds, means that he gets too close to the fence at the moment of take-off and often hits the fence with his front legs. This is a fairly common fault of the inexperienced and shows lack of judgement of stride. Place a cavalletto twenty-one feet away from the fence on the approach and this will help the horse to arrive in the correct zone for take-off.

◀ Relaxed horse on a deep bed of straw

The hoofprints of horses which went before you can be a guide to a take-off point and prevent you from taking your horse either too close to 'go through' a fence or anticipating the jump from too far off. Some horses will move and jump with a hollow back while carrying their head too high — this may be a conformation fault. Good schooling can, however, help to correct this. Working over ground rails will encourage the horse to look down to the ground with his neck stretched forwards and downwards which gives a convex or round outline.

Working on the circle, making changes of direction, using some shoulder-in, will also help to get the horse to lower his head and round his back. Lungeing with side-reins is another good training method which develops the upper line of the horse's back, by encouraging him to use the correct muscles and to find his own balance without any move on the part of the rider. There are, of course, other kinds of resistances and evasions shown by individual horses and not dealt with here. I say 'individual horses' because quite often such evasions and resistances are a matter of just that — individuality. The novice trainer who follows those training exercises which I have set down, with patience and sympathy for the 'trainee', will soon spot the idiosyncrasies of his own horse, and eliminating them from the horse's behaviour will be a matter of common sense — or, which is better, horse sense.

15. Summary

If I appear to repeat myself in the following the reader should understand that I am stressing certain points already made because they are important to bear in mind.

The three-year-old

The three-year-old horse should be so well-handled in his stable that he becomes easy to groom, trim, and lead in hand, and moves well while wearing his boots and training equipment. His schooling should occupy approximately six to eight weeks, depending on the horse's temperament which, if he is fractious in early exercises, may be due to ill-advised handling before he was introduced to the saddle and backed.

The horse should be backed towards the end of August and during early September—the process is so much easier during fair weather. At the end of the summer he should have been ridden out on hacking sessions and then turned out for the winter months. Before turning him out, however, it is advisable to have his teeth checked by the vet for sharp edges because these will make eating unpleasant, and may cause him to be unsteady in the manner of holding the bit in his mouth.

Worm the horse if it is due (see page 83), and you will have taken advice as to the nature of his pasture, bearing in mind those poisonous plants and the risk of further worm trouble in poor grazing already described. Since our British winters tend to be wet, the horse may lose condition at grass, and you may find it advisable to turn him out during the day only, bringing him in for the night. This works very well because the horse will derive the maximum value from the food he receives and by his being brought in at the end of each day it is easier for you to keep him well-mannered. During his spells in the stable you can check his general condition and brush off the mud, but do not groom him as he will need the oil and grease in his coat for warmth when in the field.

The four-year-old

Begin working him in May but first get him into condition by lungeing, long-reining and quiet hacking. In the initial stages he should be given a 'refresher course' consisting of those lessons taught during the previous year while building up his general condition. His training programme should be planned in such a way as to carry him over a period of from ten to twelve weeks — through the summer in fact. Always bear in mind the tip which I have given about that older, more experienced horse which will act as your trainee's guide and mentor and be a good example in most of his new experiences. He can be hacked out across country — on bridle paths, tracks and lanes, and also up and down slopes. As already remarked, apart from the exercise, these outings are useful in gaining experience for the young horse since during his time out he will become accustomed to sights and sounds not normally experienced in his home surroundings — to traffic, cattle and varying terrain — and, which is more important, the rider-trainer will also get to know the horse better. Working the horse over unfamiliar and uneven countryside keeps him interested and prevents boredom.

During his second week off grass you should work him over ground rails for all the training advantages already outlined. School him in his paces on turns and on circles making him respond to your leg aids. Such work can be accomplished in school or *manège* for two or three sessions a week.

In the third week of this new year cantering up and down slopes can begin, also his jumping while mounted. He may be loose-schooled over various types of fences. During the winter of his fourth year the horse can be introduced to hunting by taking him first to a cub-hunt and later hunting him for those short runs already described. During such outings he will get used to the presence of other horses and people, developing, if properly handled by his owner-trainer, both a mutual confidence and individual initiative, since he will have to encounter all kinds of 'going' — different types of country and situations.

The five-year-old

In this year the horse should be showing his potential as a dressage or show horse — perhaps a jumper or event horse. He can be taken to minor shows to compete in dressage, cross-country or hunter trials and show-jumping. A horse should not be forced to specialise until he is six to seven years old.

It must be borne in mind that a horse is still growing until well into his fifth year and must therefore receive a sound protein diet throughout. He should be turned out to graze for an hour or two each day so that he does not become bored.

Attention should always be paid to teeth and a watch kept for symptoms of worms all the year round, and the horse should have regular visits from the farrier to keep his feet in good order.

Conversion tables

Use these scales to convert feet and inches into centimetres or millimetres. Convert from feet to metres with the scale on the far right of the page. Convert inches into centimetres or millimetres by comparing the exact measurement on the inch scale with the corresponding measurement on the metric scale. For example, 1 in. equals 2·54 cm. or 25·4 mm. Similarly, 1 ft 1½ in. equals 34·3 cm. (343 mm.).

Convert centimetres or millimetres into inches by comparing the measurement on the metric scale with the corresponding unit on the inch scale. For example, 64 cm. equals 2 ft 1$\frac{3}{16}$ in., and 11 mm. equals $\frac{7}{16}$ in.

inches	mm.	inches	mm.	inches	mm.	inches	mm.	feet	metres
	1cm.	10in.	26cm.	1ft 8in.	51cm.	2ft 6in.	76cm.		
	2cm.		27cm.		52cm.		77cm.	1ft	30·5cm.
1in.	3cm.	11in.	28cm.	1ft 9in.	53cm.		78cm.		
	4cm.		29cm.		54cm.	2ft 7in.	78cm.		
2in.	5cm.	12in.	30cm.		55cm.		80cm.	2ft	61·0cm.
	6cm.		31cm.	1ft 10in.	56cm.	2ft 8in.	81cm.		
	7cm.		32cm.		57cm.		82cm.	3ft	91·4cm.
3in.	8cm.	1ft 1in.	33cm.		58cm.	2ft 9in.	83cm.	3ft 3½in.	1 metre (100cm.)
	9cm.		34cm.	1ft 11in.	59cm.		84cm.		
4in.	10cm.	1ft 2in.	35cm.		60cm.		85cm.	4ft	121·9cm.
	11cm.		36cm.	2ft	61cm.		86cm.		
	12cm.		37cm.		62cm.	2ft 10in.	87cm.		
5in.	13cm.	1ft 3in.	38cm.		63cm.		88cm.	5ft	152·4cm.
	14cm.		39cm.	2ft 1in.	64cm.	2ft 11in.	89cm.		
6in.	15cm.	1ft 4in.	40cm.		65cm.		90cm.	6ft	182·9cm.
	16cm.		41cm.	2ft 2in.	66cm.	3ft	91cm.		
	17cm.		42cm.		67cm.		92cm.	6ft 6¾in.	2 metres (200cm.)
7in.	18cm.	1ft 5in.	43cm.		68cm.		93cm.	7ft	213·4cm.
	19cm.		44cm.	2ft 3in.	69cm.	3ft 1in.	94cm.		
8in.	20cm.		45cm.		70cm.		95cm.	8ft	243·8cm.
	21cm.	1ft 6in.	46cm.	2ft 4in.	71cm.		96cm.		
	22cm.		47cm.		72cm.	3ft 2in.	97cm.		
9in.	23cm.	1ft 7in.	48cm.	2ft 5in.	73cm.		98cm.	9ft	274·3cm.
	24cm.		49cm.		74cm.	3ft 3in.	99cm.		
	25cm.		50cm.		75cm.		100cm.	9ft 10$\frac{1}{8}$in.	3 metres (300cm.)